Louis Weber, CEO
Publications International, Ltd.
7373 North Cicero Avenue
Lincolnwood, Illinois 60712

www.pilbooks.com

Permission is never granted for commercial purposes.

Manufactured in China.

8 7 6 5 4 3 2 1

ISBN-13: 978-1-4127-4051-7
ISBN-10: 1-4127-4051-7

If Cats Could Talk

THE MEANING OF MEOW

Written by Michael P. Fertig

new seasons®

But if you have me declawed,
I won't be able to do <u>this</u> anymore!

Don't try to play cute with me, mister.
I saw you out with the dog.

Just looking at me made you yawn, didn't it?

No matter what the frequency,
there's always time to dial in a little relaxation.

If you really want something,
you just have to go in and get it yourself.

When the mouse laughs at the cat,
there is a hole nearby.

–Nigerian proverb

Trust me. It'll be worth the effort.

The only thing better than a good stretch?
A good stretch in your sleep.

I am constantly amazed by my friend's
complete lack of inhibitions.

Ears. Scratch. Now.

There is no shame in not knowing…

...the shame lies in not finding out.

—Russian proverb

I'm going to close my eyes,
and when I open them
I hope there's a squeaky toy in front of me.

For your sake.

Psst. Mouse. C'mere.

I've got something to show ya.

Dog shmog.

Tell me he isn't still staring at me.

All dressed up with no place to go.

Mission: Window Shade Pull String.

Decision: Accepted.

Oh, deer!

Please do not use cosmetics or co
your hair over the wash basins.

A charge of 2p is made for use o
basin, soap and clean towel.

Towels should be returned if
fastened with a numbered ba

Bath, soap and banded towel

Sanitary towels can be obt
from the attendant, price 2

Although I look
fat and slow,
no one dares disobey
my posted rules.

I won't roll in <u>that</u> again.

Jim's Fish Market?
Do you deliver?

Find
your
place
in the
sun.
Then
take a
nap.

I trust my dinner is ready and waiting
for me in its usual spot.

Horrible conflict?
Or two unlikely friends
playing a game?

How many dogs does it take
to screw in a light bulb?
All of 'em.
One to turn it, and the rest
to run around in circles and bark at it!

You are getting sleepy.

Your eyelids are getting heavy.

You want to give me a big can of tuna.

Canine Control 101.

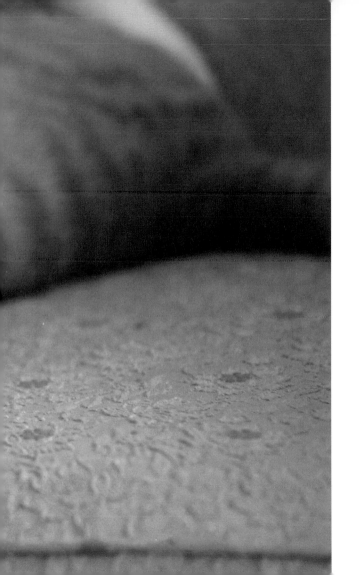

After a long
day of lying
on the sofa,
I like to unwind
by rolling over
for a stretch
and a nap.

Who says bad things happen in threes?

Then you
shouldn't have
put the
dinner rolls
in <u>my</u>
basket.

Then is it <u>good</u> luck if I cross your path?

Nothing beats curbside service.

Hard day. Hair ball. Nuff said.

One should be just as careful
in choosing one's pleasures
as in avoiding calamities.

–Chinese proverb

Do <u>not</u> sneak up on me like that.

It isn't the size of the human.
It's the size of the love in the human.

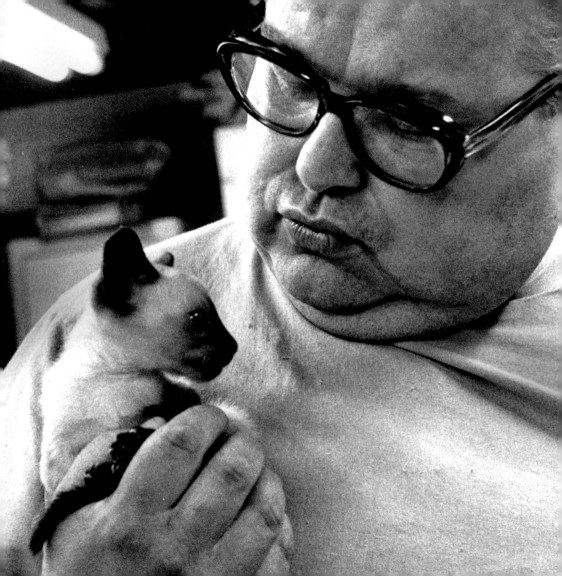